Our Own Society

Daryl V. Hoole

Photography by Libby Frech

Bookcraft
Salt Lake City, Utah

Salt Lake City, Utah

Library of Congress Catalog Card Number: 79-63403
ISBN 0-88494-366-6
First Printing, 1979

Lithographed in the United States of America
PUBLISHERS PRESS
Salt Lake City, Utah

ACKNOWLEDGMENTS

Projects such as writing a book are made more successful through the confidence, counsel, and encouragement of special people in the author's life. For me, these very helpful people have been my husband, H.J.M. Hoole, Jr.; my mother, Ada S. Van Dam; two close friends, Jeri Lynn H. Horman and Kaye R. Rollins; and my counselors in our ward Relief Society presidency, Margaret J. Pahnke and Marcie C. Alley.

I deeply appreciate Libby Frech, whom I met in Columbus, Ohio, and her contribution to this book through her sensitive photography. I am delighted her gift as an artist with the camera can be shared in this way.

I owe a special debt of gratitude to the Relief Society sisters of the Church, particularly those of Yalecrest Second Ward, Salt Lake Bonneville Stake, for the inspiration which made this book possible.

CONTENTS

That
Relief Society
Feeling

It happens differently for each woman. In my case, the warm, good feeling I've developed for Relief Society goes back to an experience I had when I was four years old. It was during the 1930s, when Relief Society bazaars were held, and I can still vividly recall attending one with my parents.

I remember the tasty hot chili and the ice cold milk we had for dinner. There was a "fish pond" where children "caught" all sorts of fascinating trinkets. And I can still picture the array of brightly colored quilts and aprons which were on sale. How delighted I was when my parents purchased a little patchwork quilt with a blue backing for my doll. I was an only child at that time, and my doll was my

best friend and playmate. For years I tucked her into bed each night with that treasured quilt.

Ever since then, thoughts of Relief Society have been synonymous with the happy, warm, good things of life. In fact, the very name **Relief Society** causes a parade of pleasant thoughts to go through my mind. Even as a little girl, I sensed that it represented something very important and meaningful to me. I knew I wanted to make it a vital part of my life as my mother was doing.

It was some years later before I realized specifically what role Relief Society would play in my life. Until I married and became active in Relief Society for myself, it was the purpose I sensed rather than the program which convinced me that it was for me.

And this is all right, because the program has changed. Over the years it has grown to meet the needs of the times. But its divinely inspired ideals, which foster sisterhood, service, personal growth, strengthening the home and community, and conversion to gospel principles, remain the same.

I have seen Relief Society grow from an organization wherein interested women could enjoy membership by paying annual dues, to a fully priesthood-directed and -supported program which includes every woman of the Church as a member.

This is as it was intended to be. On March 17, 1842, the Prophet Joseph Smith organized "the Female Relief Society of Nauvoo" after the pattern of the priesthood. On that occasion the Prophet said, "The Church was never

perfectly organized until the women were thus organized."
(Relief Society Magazine, March 1919, page 129.) At a
later time he gave this specific counsel to those sisters:

> Let this society teach women how to behave towards
> their husbands, to treat them with mildness and
> affection. When a man is borne down with trouble,
> when he is perplexed with care and difficulty, if he
> can meet a smile instead of an argument or a mur-
> mur — if he can meet with mildness it will calm down
> his soul and soothe his feelings; when the mind is
> going to despair it needs a solace of affection and
> kindness. (Documentary History of the Church,
> vol. 4, pages 606-607.)

Later, at the second Relief Society meeting of the
Church, Lucy Mack Smith, the Prophet's mother, said,
"We must cherish one another, watch over one another;
and gain instruction, that we may all sit down in heaven
together." (Relief Society Minutes, March 24, 1842.)

What was once eighteen women in Nauvoo, Illinois,
has become now more than a million women in Tokyo,
Buenos Aires, Salt Lake City, Brussels, Honolulu, Los
Angeles, Sydney, and Anchorage — almost all over the
world.

There are other women's organizations — some also
worldwide — which have lofty goals and high aspirations,
but the Relief Society is the only women's organization
anywhere which is directed by the priesthood of God. It is
the counterpart to the priesthood. The goals and purposes of this organization, therefore, take on special significance as we consider them.

These goals and purposes, as taken from the 1968 Relief Society Handbook of Instructions, are —

1. to manifest benevolence;
2. to care for the poor, the sick, and the unfortunate;
3. to minister where death reigns;
4. to give guidance and training in the homemaking arts and skills;
5. to assist in correcting the morals and strengthening the virtues of community life;
6. to raise human life to its highest level;
7. to elevate and enlarge the scope of women's activities and conditions;
8. to foster love for religion, education, culture, and refinement;
9. to develop faith;
10. to save souls;
11. to study and teach the gospel.

With our motto **charity** and our slogan **service**, we are engaged in what matters most in life. A short verse, given in a **Relief Society Magazine** (February 1950), outlines our all-encompassing role as women in the Church:

> Woman's sphere is bounded only
> By the talents God has given,
> And her duty lies wherever
> Earth can be made more like heaven.

Every Relief Society experience I have reaffirms that warm, good feeling I felt as a four-year-old at the bazaar. I will be eternally grateful that I decided to make Relief Society a vital part of my life. I love it. I believe in it. Next to being at home with my husband and children, I am happier being involved in Relief Society-centered activities than anything else. Through the following pages I'd like to explain why and how.

Finding Time
for Relief Society

If anyone should ever ask me to tell them in twenty-five words or less how, along with managing the home and serving our family, I'm able to give many hours of service to Relief Society, I would answer, "It's because of a 'foundation' theory I practice, the list-making habit I have, and the cooperation and support which my husband and children give me." I'd like to discuss these three facets in detail.

As important as service to our fellowmen at large is, service to our families is, of course, of far greater significance. I don't ever want to be accused of being a better neighbor or Relief Society worker than I am a wife, mother, and homemaker.

To ensure this, I compare my daily home management to building a house, which has a cornerstone, a foundation, and then a structure. I feel that the cornerstone is me, the wife and mother. I find it vital for my own mental health and the positive feelings of everyone else concerned that I look and feel as good as possible. "Beauty is a duty!" (We wives and mothers might even copy that slogan on a card and place it in our dressing rooms.)

Everyone knows that an attractive physical appearance and good health come about, to a large extent, through personal grooming and exercise and proper food and rest. We further know that emotional and spiritual well-being are a result of prayer, scripture searching, meditation, note making, and keeping the commandments.

It's when mom looks good and feels well and is close to the Lord that everything functions best at home. It can mean a great deal to a woman to have all these components of the cornerstone in place every day.

The "foundation" phase of this building project is to quickly put our homes in order early each morning. This includes routine duties such as making beds, serving and clearing up breakfast, cleaning the bathroom, washing and folding clothes, and tidying up throughout the house. (It does not include extended phone calls, newspaper reading, TV watching, or cleaning out closets early in the morning.)

When I have our family house in order each day, my work really starts. It's exciting at that point to see how high and how well I can build the "structure" that day. This is where a lot of Relief Society activities and service enter in. Now that my children are all in school and are a little more independent, I can often spend several hours a day in such out-of-the-home activities.

I've learned through some real life experiences that it's better and easier in the long run to attend to this "foundation" phase than it is not to do it. Even in those days when babies came along regularly and I often was suffering from morning sickness, I found it easier to get out of bed, no matter how I felt, and almost crawl to the kitchen and prepare breakfast than to let four preschoolers get the food for themselves. I learned that it was smart to clear the table immediately after eating. Otherwise a toddler could climb up, scatter sugar, pour milk over his head, and polish the kitchen with butter. Similarly, I learned that it was a lot easier to fold each batch of clothing as it came out of the dryer than to let it mound up and then try to find two matching socks for someone.

I've observed over the years that all women who manage their homes well and who accomplish a lot in a day's time follow this procedure of cornerstone, foundation, and structure. Many of them aren't aware of what they're doing — they've never really analyzed their efforts or put labels or names on them, but that is their system nevertheless. Some women call it by a different name. I have a friend who refers to her morning routine as "the big five." She does "the big five" every morning before she leaves her home or becomes involved in other projects and pursuits. This is in keeping with family expectations.

It's every woman's challenge to learn to complete these tasks, through her personal efficiency and with the help of family members, early each morning. Then, upon such a foundation, it's exciting to see how high and well she can build the rest of the day. She can go on to a deeper cleaning, cooking, baking, sewing, mending, gardening, decorating, personal projects, Church work, community service, and child guidance. (Child care is part of the foundation; child guidance is building at its very best.)

I believe that, as husbands and children return home each day after their work and schooling, they hope to find a happy wife and mother; a clean, orderly home; and a tasty, nutritious dinner. If Mother also attended Relief Society or spent half the day in Relief Society service, or if she planted some vegetables or flowers, prepared a lesson, attended a class, did some reading and studying, went to a luncheon, or took the children to the zoo, they are happy for her and glad she had a nice day too.

Should family members, however, come home to a frustrated wife and mother, a disorderly, neglected house, and a starvation meal, they might resent her activities of the day, regardless of how worthwhile these may have been. To foster in husbands and children any negative attitudes toward Relief Society and its related service is certainly something we never want to do.

Instead, our husbands and children should learn through our efforts that obligations to Relief Society cause us to schedule, organize, and manage even better in our homes. Relief Society commitments, kept in control and in proper proportions, provide some healthy, motivating deadlines for us women. The information, inspiration, and ideas gained in Relief Society classes often bring about such enthusiasm and motivation in our own lives that we can work faster and more efficiently as a result. Deadlines and assignments set us in motion. Ideas provide fuel for one's self-starter, and Relief Society is a wonderful place to exchange ideas.

We want our family members to feel that because of Relief Society we as wives and mothers are more enthusiastic and exciting, more informed and interesting, and more capable and qualified people than we would otherwise be. We want them to realize that we are more converted and committed to the gospel because of what we learn at Relief Society. All of this makes our homes better places to be.

As we practice this "foundation" theory, family members will know that they are number one in our lives. It then becomes easy for them to readily accept and benefit from our secondary activities.

Our children are young investigators of the gospel, waiting to be converted. And this conversion, I feel, largely comes through making the gospel work at home. It's through a loving, caring home, where happiness and harmony prevail and where parents have their priorities in order, that children will embrace the parents' values. When children like their parents, they are more likely to like what the parents believe.

Of course, in the lives of us women as neighbors and

Relief Society members, there are times when emergencies arise, causing us to rush to attend to them without regard to a "cornerstone" or a "foundation." We do such things as take ill people to the hospital in the early hours of the morning, spend the night in the home of a sister who is too sick to stay alone, or bathe or dress someone who cannot help herself. We sometimes drop everything to prepare food or otherwise help someone in need. But when such crises come up, children and husbands will usually rise to the occasion and put forth extra effort at home to relieve the mother. They, too, catch the spirit of service.

The problem is that some mothers declare emergencies every day. All too often, mothers bring unnecessary difficulties on themselves. They, and not circumstances, are the disaster! The husband and children of such a woman soon lose interest. A smart mother manages so that when a real emergency comes up she has a reservoir of good will on the part of family members from which she can draw.

The second facet of finding time for Relief Society in my life is note making. Putting plans, appointments, menus, thoughts, and ideas on paper is my answer to the problem of getting things done. I find that few things motivate me quite like a list of duties and projects, and almost nothing calms and relaxes me quite like that list completed and crossed off. I find, too, that I can keep track of and follow up on an amazing number of activities through my lists without feeling tense or rushed. It helps me immensely to put the pressure on paper, rather than

on my mind. Once something is on my list, I keep working at it until it finally gets done. Sometimes I have to list something a half-dozen times or more and go back time and again before I get to or complete it, but sooner or later its turn comes. With such organization, there is time for everything — eventually. To prevent my lists from being lost or scattered, I keep them conveniently contained in a little notebook which I carry in my purse, so they are always with me for reference at any time, any place.

Along with a schedule of meetings and assignments and things to do and buy, it's a good idea to keep lists of names of people who could benefit from a little help or encouragement. You can call some of these sisters on the phone while you're folding clothes, mending, or preparing a casserole. It's rewarding to visit while you work, and others seem to appreciate the call. It's remarkable how many lives you can touch in this manner without taking any actual time from family responsibilities. Another list could remind you of those who need a personal visit — shut-ins, lonely people, and new neighbors.

A significant aspect of these lists is that they can free one's mind from the clutter of too many details and thoughts so that the Spirit can nudge when someone whose name is not on the list needs help that day.

As you bake and cook, you can share goodies with those who would benefit from such a thoughtful gesture. I realized how important it is, however, to always give our first consideration to our families when, one day, a child in our family entered the kitchen, noticed that I was baking, and promptly asked, "Who's sick?" Suddenly I wondered what kind of an impression I was giving our family. Did I bake only when someone needed help? I realized it would be better to bake for the family and share part of it than to bake for someone else and let the family eat a little of it too.

One husband said, "I often smell cookies when I get home after work, but I never can find any." He would appreciate his wife reserving part of the batch for him.

It happens that my daughters bake and cook nearly as much for school functions and friends as I do for the Relief Society. We have agreed that at least half of whatever we produce in our kitchen remains home for the family. Husbands and sons, particularly, seem to appreciate this. Fifty percent of it is always for the family! (Of course, there can be exceptions to this when large amounts of food are prepared for some purpose, but the general rule holds.)

This brings me to the third facet in budgeting my time and arranging my life to include Relief Society. That is the cooperation and support of my husband and children. They're great in this way, and I try to let them know it. I couldn't do much extra at all without their help, support, and encouragement.

Through various expressions of appreciation, we are able to tell family members what their cooperation means to us. They will come to realize that if we all help one another, each one of us can do and serve and progress more. It's gratifying to see how family members can add to one another's effectiveness and efficiency.

For example, our children should work with us as we lay the foundation of routine housework each morning. What a great help it can be to have children leave their bedrooms and bathrooms clean and orderly each morning and also give some assistance with the dishes and dusting, carrying out the trash, and feeding the pets! Learning to set a "cornerstone" and lay a "foundation" before children try to build their "structure" is a good pattern for their lives as well as ours. They, too, will be delighted with how high and well they can build as a result.

Just as the family helps each child, each child should help the family. Everyone needs to assist with the work in the home just as everyone enjoys the shelter, food, clothing, transportation, and other opportunities provided there. The secret to this type of teamwork on the part of family members is to establish early in children's lives the habits of neatness, helpfulness, respect, and thoughtfulness.

It's helpful to make lists of duties for each child, just as we do for ourselves, until they are mature enough to make their own lists. Lists are a constructive way to bring about family teamwork, and they also give children the satisfaction of making plans and carrying them out. Lists also eliminate nagging and interrupting on mother's part. Lists help a mother keep track of little jobs which little children can handle; otherwise such things as wiping spots and fingerprints from the front and back doors are neglected. Furthermore, lists are black-and-white evidence

of what everyone is supposed to do. No one can sneak off without doing his part. And lists systematize household responsibilities and help to get things done. Otherwise it's a matter of hit and miss — everyone running about, with very little really accomplished.

And best of all about lists — they help establish good habits and self-discipline in our lives. Many duties can become routine acts, hardly any thought or concern being given to them. At this point, one's "automatic pilot" can take over and emphasis can be put on higher levels of living and working and serving.

Children can assist mother in baking and cooking for other people and in various service projects. Cooking can be great fun, and when children help they can also learn the joy of sharing and serving. Children can accompany the mother as she takes food to people. Often she cannot carry all of it alone and she really does need their help.

A young woman from Salt Lake City told me that when she was ten years old her mother became the ward Relief Society president. She accompanied her mother on many compassionate service activities, and this helped her learn the importance of sisterly love. Later, when she was a member of the Young Adult Relief Society session, she became her mother's visiting teaching partner. In this way she learned early in her life how to be a caring, compassionate visiting teacher. She caught the spirit of the work through a dedicated mother.

I must say at this point, however, that, as helpful as all the foregoing philosophy has been to me personally over the years, it doesn't always work. When I had babies, toddlers, and preschool children, I was a 50 percent attender at Relief Society due to runny noses, a sudden rash on someone, or a baby who chose to scream rather than sleep on my lap. There are times when, in spite of a mother's best efforts, she cannot get to Relief Society. Through consistent and conscientious efforts, though, her chances are a lot better.

Sometimes I arrived at the meeting late because an interrupted night had caused a slow start that morning, or a last-minute, unexpected diaper change had delayed me. Once in a while, removing sand from a two-year-old's hair or mud from his shoes really slowed me down.

By the time our eldest child was seven, we had six children. Those years were not easy or smooth ones. But I especially needed at that time what Relief Society offered. I made a big effort to get there as often as possible. So that I could attend, sometimes during those demanding years my husband prepared breakfast and assisted me in other ways. He felt and feels much the same as the husband did in the following excerpt from a home teaching message, prepared by Barbara K. Christensen, for the Salt Lake Bonneville Stake: "I do everything I can to ensure that my wife will be able to attend Relief Society, because I am convinced that she **and** we really benefit. She learns so much that helps us in the home, both in our relationship with each other and with the children. Her life is enriched by the Spirit, and that is a source of strength for us all. It takes a little cooperation from all of us, but we make sure that she can be involved. We know it is for her and **our** good. Also, I feel confident that our efforts now will have a great effect for good in the future lives and homes of our daughters and sons. There is a much greater chance that Relief Society will bless their lives and homes years from now because they will have experienced its impact for good today. It may take a little effort to schedule, encourage, and plan and to make special meal arrangements some days, or whatever, but it's worth it."

There are women who use responsibilities at home as an excuse to stay away from Relief Society. They are cheating themselves and their families, I feel. Of course, as I said earlier, there are occasions when illnesses and other circumstances interfere with a mother's attendance at Relief Society, and justifiably so, but I believe that on a normal basis a person finds the time to do whatever she wants to do. Opportunity and determination often travel together.

As well as women who excuse themselves from Relief Society because of home responsibilities, other women, unfortunately, use Relief Society responsibilities as an excuse to neglect matters at home. They rationalize their problems away or justify a messy, neglected house by saying, "Oh, but I was helping someone else." For them, Church and community service are an escape. They, too, are cheating themselves and their families.

Actually, it can be easier to be a good Relief Society officer or teacher than to be a good wife, mother, and homemaker. It can be a lot simpler to be organized at

Relief Society than it is at home. It's easier to talk about it and teach it than it is to do it! The test is at home — the real proving ground.

Success in one sphere, however, need not detract from success in another. Actually, the same principles that make us effective in our Church assignments will help us at home. One responsibility can supplement the other.

I don't believe that either the totally-devoted-to-one's-family philosophy or the escape attitude are in keeping with what our Father in heaven wants for us as women of the Church. I am convinced that through the development of self-discipline and some basic skills we can be loving wives, effective mothers, skilled homemakers, and devoted Relief Society sisters. Thousands of women are doing this, and countless blessings are theirs as a result.

It's usually the mother who sets the emotional temperature of the household and determines the cultural and spiritual quality of family members' lives. If she is happy, she helps the people around her to be happy too. But if her "well runs dry," so to speak, she has nothing to give anyone else. I am convinced that the Relief Society organization is the means whereby our Father in heaven can "refill" the well of the mothers of Zion in this dispensation. It is his plan and program for us. Through it we are able to receive in a most wholesome, ideal way, that we might in turn give in the same manner.

I notice there are two extreme philosophies prevailing among some women today. Some feel they should sacrifice everything for the sake of their families. As a good neighbor of mine put it, "Sometimes a woman sacrifices herself to the point that she actually sacrifices herself." In the name of being a good wife and mother, such women deny themselves service opportunities, growth experiences, and stimulating activities outside the home. These women are maids, not mates and mothers. They slave for their families rather than serve them. They come to feel they are martyrs, and eventually resentment and bitterness creep into their lives. Husbands and children regard them as "doormats" and tend to lose respect for them.

The other extreme philosophy which is becoming alarmingly prevalent in today's world is that of "do your own thing." This attitude gives sanction and license to some women to think only of themselves; and in a very selfish, worldly way they neglect or entirely abandon their families and homes. Certainly this is a path to destruction and is a diabolical concept which sometimes deceives the very elect.

Somewhere between almost total indulgence to a family and "doing your own thing" is an ideal approach to being a wife, mother, homemaker, and woman. Blessed is the LDS woman who realizes there is an answer to this through the gospel of Jesus Christ, particularly in the Relief Society program. As individuals and as families, we may be eternally blessed because of this perspective.

Of course, we must be sensible about the service we render. Helping others, no matter how worthwhile the cause might be, is not worth it if one's own family and home are neglected in the process or if one's health is jeopardized. We must never run faster than we have strength. We can sometimes become so caught up in a good cause that we forget what our true purpose is. We have to guard against allowing worthy projects or well-intentioned people to take over our lives. Sometimes it's important that a mother say **no** to someone else so she can say **yes** to her family. The gospel teaches us moderation in all things. We may have to get on our knees to find where we should draw the line.

But when principles of self-discipline and good home management are applied and when circumstances are normal, there is usually time for both family and Relief Society.

The Mormon Mother Image

One time when I was giving some home management lectures in California a woman approached me and said she was a convert to the Church. She told me how she loved its teachings. Then she added: "It wasn't too difficult for us to learn to live the gospel. We've always been good Christian people, and joining the Church didn't cause too many adjustments in our living. Learning to live the Word of Wisdom, paying tithing, keeping the Sabbath Day holy, and serving in our ward and stake found their places quite naturally in our lives. My challenge has been in learning how to be the ideal LDS mother and homemaker."

She went on to say: "You women are amazing. I cannot believe all that a Mormon mother does. Why, before I joined the Church I had never seen bread dough; I didn't know fruit could be bottled at home; I had never used a sewing machine; and the thoughts of having a baby every year or so seemed incredible to me." Such feelings, I've discovered, are echoed by many women everywhere. Of course, not all converts feel this way, but a great number of them do.

Frequently women who have been members of the Church all their lives confess to me the challenges they feel in living up to the standards the Church has set for the home and family. They often feel overwhelmed and inadequate, discouraged and depressed. Not being able to live up to the ideal, in their estimation, sometimes causes them to suffer from the "Mormon Mother Syndrome." This, of course, is a self-defeating pattern. Discouragement is one of the most commonly used tools of the adversary. It opens the door to many other problems. Self-pity saps a person's strength. It can make a woman tired and sick and thereby highly vulnerable to a long list of negative attitudes and destructive feelings. Some women who are above temptation in other areas fall prey to the devil's devices for causing them to feel discouraged. These women need a great deal of help, instruction, and encouragement. I feel this can largely come through Relief Society.

Numerous lessons and programs focus on helping women improve their homemaking skills. Lessons on basic time management are taught. Instruction on how to budget money is given. Hints, recipes, and ideas are shared. Cooking and sewing skills are taught and practiced. The best in child guidance techniques are discussed. Ideas for improving family relations are presented. Ways to beautify the home are suggested. In this environment attitudes are caught; examples are evidenced; the spirit of learning, growing, improving, and conquering permeates. Miracles take place in mothers' lives.

Occasionally a woman says the Relief Society curriculum depresses her. She feels she cannot incorporate into her life all that is taught and demonstrated there. I can't either! And it is not intended that any one sister develop an expertise in every class topic presented at Relief Society. For instance, mini-classes on homemaking day are to be regarded as a smorgasbord of ideas where each woman selects what appeals and applies to her life. There is far more offered than any one woman could use, but the variety and selection are exciting and stimulating.

A woman need not employ all the homemaking skills at one time in her life in order to feel she is being a good mother and homemaker. After applying the basics of good housekeeping and good family living, she is free to add or ignore other touches according to her talents, abilities, circumstances, and needs. It makes some women nervous and irritable to sew. Perhaps they should leave the sewing to someone else and merely keep up the mending at home. It's more economical for some women to teach a few music lessons in their homes in order to buy new furniture than attempt to refinish or recover old pieces. Some

women don't care for feather flowers or macrame; they would prefer other types of decor in their homes. That's as it should be — how dull and uninteresting it would be if all our homes looked alike! Of a dozen ideas suggested to enrich the lives of children, perhaps only three or four of them fit your personality and situation. But Relief Society offers many options so women can make intelligent choices.

A wise LDS woman will center her thinking around all that she can do, rather than that which she cannot do. With such confidence she will feel challenged, rather than threatened, when new fields of growth and development are opened up to her.

Furthermore, some skills taught at Relief Society are for "storage" in the event they might be needed at some future date. For example, normally I use only a small fraction of the information I learned through the home nursing instructions, but the knowledge I gained and tucked away in a corner of my mind could make the difference between comfort or suffering, life or death some day. And in case I forget some information along the way, I still have the lesson manual on file.

As a general rule, we tend to enjoy most hearing about what we do best. That's our comfort zone. I once attended a Relief Society mini-class on diet and weight control. As I looked around the group, I could tell by the expressions on the women's faces that the ones who enjoyed the lesson most were the trim ones!

There are other reasons which cause some women to

return home from a meeting dejected rather than lifted up. I know of one woman, Beth, who has become very interested in the Church through her neighbor and is eager to be baptized. She is deeply sorrowed, however, by the fact that her husband does not share her interest in the gospel and refuses to discuss it. She attended a Relief Society lesson in the mother education department where family traditions were discussed, but the wonderful ideas and suggestions presented brought her to the point of tears. How could she get excited about special events connected with holidays and various family activities when her husband wouldn't allow even the most basic traditions such as blessings over the food and family prayers. She felt her family situation was hopeless. She wished she hadn't attended Relief Society that morning and been reminded how bereft their living was of meaningful experiences. She felt like giving up, telling herself that they would never make it.

It was only through the encouragement of her LDS neighbor that she was able to turn her despair into some constructive thinking and acting. Her neighbor pointed out that they did have some traditions as a family. Didn't she see her husband pitching balls to their boys many evenings after dinner? Didn't the whole family get in the car almost every Saturday morning to watch one of the children play soccer? They talked on and the list of their good times together began to grow.

It would be important for her to start where they were, with what they were already doing, and be grateful for that. She should dwell on her husband's good points — and there were many of them — and let him know of her appreciation and acceptance. She should make the most of each moment and not allow what they were not doing to detract from what they were doing. And then through a lot of faith and prayer and tender loving care, who knows what can happen to the husband! Miracles take place in people's lives every day. There are thousands of stories in the Church about hard hearts that have been softened.

Some women are made to feel uncomfortable by what they hear at Church meetings. Talks and lessons which discuss divorce, wayward children and other unhappy situations remind them of their problems and heartaches and add to their feelings of remorse and guilt. The tendency in some cases is for women to avoid meetings, to withdraw from situations which disturb them. This is a terribly destructive approach, as such feelings destroy faith, making two problems out of one.

Even though it could be extremely difficult to develop such feelings, a much more constructive, Christlike attitude would be to attend meetings with the conviction that through supporting and participating, encouraging and sharing, you might help someone else avoid the same pitfalls. A little of the hurt in your heart over a recalcitrant child could be lessened with the knowledge that you had helped several other young people find their way.

In the process you are keeping yourself strong and close to the Lord and his representatives on earth. Through proper worship and constant activity in the Church, you are putting on the whole armor of God. You are growing in wisdom and understanding, strength and righteousness. You may learn to live above your problems. You might even find the key which will solve your problems.

And somewhere, someone else doing the same thing might help your loved one.

It was President David O. McKay who stated, "No other success can compensate for failure in the home." We have not failed, however, until we have given up. Full activity in Church programs, including Relief Society, is an indication that you are still trying.

A friend of mine in a neighboring ward was asked by her bishop and Relief Society president to be the mother education teacher, but she was very reluctant to accept the calling. She had a heavy heart due to a wayward son and felt that preparing and presenting lessons on success-ful child guidance would be more than she could bear. Her problems with her son caused her to feel unworthy and in-competent for the assignment. She felt she could not be an effective teacher or a good example under such circum-stances. The bishop urged her, however, to accept the call, promising her peace in her life and blessings in her home. She followed his counsel.

During one of the lessons that year a grateful sister in the group happened to bear testimony to the fact that through praying and fasting her daughter had been able to overcome some problems. The teacher felt she understood well the principles of prayer and fasting, and she was familiar with how Alma the Elder had influenced the Lord to cause an angel to get the attention of his son as a direct result of his faith and that of his people. But somehow that day the meaning of praying and fasting in behalf of someone else came to her with such force that she knew at that moment it was the means to the blessings she so desperately needed. The impact of the message was like a personal revelation to her.

Of course she had been praying for her son all along, but that day she committed herself to an intense program of praying mightily to the Lord, fasting one day a week, and keeping the boy's name in the temple. Instead of weeping over him and worrying about him, she started exercising faith and doing positive works. Her husband joined her in this. Little by little things began to change. Within two years the boy had put his life in order and was bringing his parents the joys and blessings of an honorable son.

Because of a positive influence at Relief Society, this woman was able to put into practice a life-changing principle, one that I heard Stephen R. Covey emphasize in a talk: "There is no greater way to bless another person than to pray with him and for him in a believing attitude. It can help open up the powers of heaven in that person's life."

I know this to be true. Through praying and fasting we can bring about righteous changes in others. We can find the way to personal improvement and growth and strength in ourselves, thereby coming closer to that Mormon Mother Image. A loving Father in heaven is eager to

help us if we will just allow him to do so. If we do our absolute best, then his will can be done, according to what he knows is most beneficial for us.

Sister Barbara B. Smith, general president of the Relief Society, was speaking before a group of women when one of the sisters asked her why the expectations for Relief Society sisters were so high. Sister Smith answered: "The program is built upon our strengths, not our weaknesses. Its purpose is to cause us to grow, not to sit back and find comfort in our deficiencies."

It's been said there is no progress without pain. Lessons and sermons are given to stir us and (we hope) motivate us to growth and progress. The programs of the Church are not to discourage, but rather to build. We must allow this to happen.

The standards of the Church are high. It takes some tall stretching to reach them. The path to perfection involves overcoming ourselves and our environment. It involves fulfilling our stewardship and magnifying our callings as wives, mothers, and homemakers. It requires service to our Father in heaven through service to our fellowmen. It means becoming Christlike.

All of this requires a lot of hard work. But I like to think that the gospel does not work us to death, it works us to life — even to eternal life. And in striving to measure up, we have the assurance of the prophet Nephi's promise: "I will go and do the things which the Lord hath commanded, for I know that the Lord giveth no commandments unto the children of men, save he shall prepare a way for them that they may accomplish the thing which he commandeth them." (1 Nephi 3:7.)

What It's All About

"Mommy, is it time for 'Reesy Siety'?" or, "Let's go to 'Wa Yeef Society'" are common cries from little children who may not know how to pronounce the words, but who do know that an enjoyable, constructive time awaits them at Relief Society nursery.

Thousands of young children throughout the Church feel that attending Relief Society nurseries is one of their favorite activities of the week. In fact, they can be so enthusiastic about being there that they have been known to push a hesitant mother right out of the house on her way to the meeting. Some children even get the notion that the whole Relief Society program revolves around the nursery and that everything has been set up just for them. When our youngest was five years old, I once told him I couldn't go to Relief Society that morning. Much to my surprise, he reached for his coat and quickly replied: "Oh, that's all right. I won't be gone long." I started to protest, but he interrupted me by saying, "Don't feel bad, Mom, I'll bring home everything I make so you can see it." It almost took force to restrain him that morning.

It is much more enjoyable for adults and infinitely more rewarding for children when children are taught, rather than merely tended. At Relief Society nurseries, children are taught. There is a learning program designed just for them in which they are instructed in gospel principles, beautiful and interesting things in the world around them, music and rhythm, stories and poetry, arts and crafts, and constructive play activities. And even more important than what they learn is what they do. For almost two hours they participate in sharing, learning, playing, eating, and getting along together. A nursery program such as this is like the world in miniature — a child learns much about living through such a setting. It can be most beneficial for him to attend this one morning a week.

The word **nursery** doesn't really do justice to what actually takes place. The term **Child Teaching Society** is much more appropriate. Instead of a paid baby-sitter in charge, as used to be the case, the program is now directed and supervised by coordinators of the calibre of Primary presidents and is handled by teams of mothers who pool their talents and resources and take turns in the nursery to give each child a happy, meaningful experience.

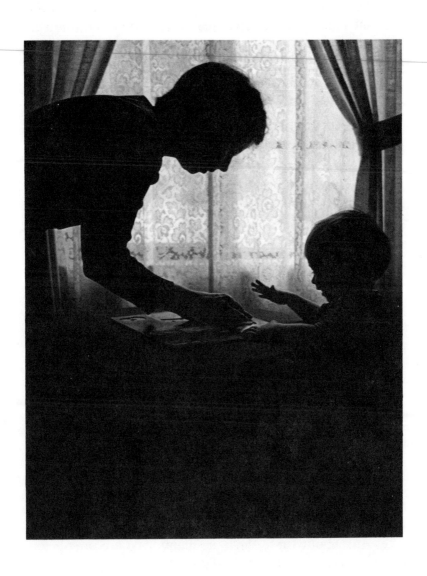

The growth of the nursery program, however, is only a small indication of what has happened to the entire Relief Society organization. If children are happy, their mothers, aunts, sisters, and grandmothers are even happier with what has taken place.

Many changes have allowed the Relief Society to expand its capabilities of reaching individual sisters by allowing them to serve and "be served." For example, as late as 1967 every ward Relief Society organization held one meeting a week. It required a team of ten to twelve women to staff each group. Lessons were presented in theology, social science, and literature. A visiting teaching message was given, and a monthly "work day" was conducted.

Now the program has been expanded to the point where many wards of the Church hold at least three sessions of Relief Society each week. There is a session held on a weekday morning, and another one meets on an evening during the week or early Sunday morning for women who are not free to attend the weekday morning session. In addition, women aged eighteen to twenty-six get together at a time of their choice for the Young Adult session. Some wards add other sessions, such as one for patients in a nursing home.

Officers and teachers required to direct and instruct these sessions now number from twenty-two to thirty-five women. Thus, about three times as many women as in 1967 now have the opportunity to grow through service. And about three times as many lives are now being touched through this enlarged program.

In the case of small branch units, however, a mini-staff may function comprising only a portion of the usual number of officers and teachers. The basic structure can be adapted to fit any situation, anywhere the Church is organized in the world. It is an inspired, universal program capable of meeting the needs of women of the Church everywhere.

The basic Relief Society lesson courses are still taught, though their names have changed a little. Today they are known as spiritual living, social relations, and cultural refinement. Mother education has been added. The visiting teaching message endures.

The most dramatic change, however, has been from the old work day to the new homemaking day. It has progressed remarkably from what used to be mainly a quilting bee or sewing circle to a vibrant, dynamic, many-faceted meeting designed to meet the needs of women everywhere. A short but pertinent lesson is presented on homemaking or a related subject such as home nursing. Through these practical lessons the quality of a woman's homemaking can be greatly enhanced.

The follow-up and practical application of these brief lessons comes next. At its close, women are divided into smaller groups to attend the mini-class of their choice. The remainder of the day is filled with a variety of mini-classes from which Relief Society sisters select the class they wish to attend. And what a selection there is — everything from crepe suzette making to hair cutting, from understanding the metric system to writing one's life story.

In fact, the only limit to the classes is one's imagination. As members of the Church we seek "anything virtuous, lovely, or of good report or praiseworthy." These are certainly the criteria for mini-classes.

A Relief Society member from Oregon says that through a mini-class on doing serious things on sunny days she learned how to set up a family trust.

A convert to the Church in California says that she was the proverbial bride who didn't even know how to boil water or warm the soup without burning it. She credits Relief Society for teaching her how to be a good cook. Now she even gives sourdough demonstrations because an interest in this was encouraged at Relief Society. She further reports that her sister-in-law learned to sew at Relief Society, and then taught her that skill. She sums up her feelings by saying, "In a world where women are encouraged to 'do their own thing' and coming from an environment where this attitude was especially prevalent, I have learned that there is great peace and satisfaction in doing what we are supposed to do."

Often an attractive, tasty, nutritious luncheon is served at the close of the homemaking day activities in the case of the weekday Relief Society session. (This custom is altered for the evening or Sunday morning sessions.) The good food, recipe exchanges, attractive table arrangements, and socializing make this a highlight of the month's activities.

"Every time I prepare and serve a new dish at home," says a sister from Idaho, "I try hard to have my family believe that I am a 'super' cook, but they have all figured out that it's really that I attended Relief Society during the week and have just copied the menu and used the same recipes."

Of course, not every effort brings success, and sometimes learning and experience come the hard way. One young woman baked some zucchini bread for a Young Adult Relief Society function. It wasn't until she saw the reaction of the group that she learned that "1 tsp. B.P." on the recipe card meant baking powder, not black pepper.

Several times a year the homemaking day luncheon progresses to a full-scale social in honor of Christmas, the anniversary of the organization of Relief Society in March of 1842, or some other occasion. Clever themes, appealing invitations, attractive decorations, and entertaining programs mark these events. These occasions further challenge and develop the talents of the sisters. Frequently all the sessions of one ward get together for a joint social, which promotes sisterhood and a feeling of unity among the women of the ward. Once in a while husbands are also invited to attend an evening social. This active interest on the part of priesthood bearers is much appreciated, and many of the brethren have been known to concede that the sisters really do have a corner on outstanding meetings.

Relief Society has long been compared to a great continuing education program. In fact, the knowledge gained there over the years can be equated with a college liberal arts degree. Actually, I'd rather learn at Relief Society because all the chaff has been sifted out of the material presented and only the pure kernels of truth are left.

A northern California sister told me about her experience with Relief Society: "Early in my marriage I began attending our community college. I loved it! My older sister tried to tell me that I could get the same education at Relief Society. I laughed! I thought she was 'nuts.' About six years ago a smart homemaking leader called on me to teach a mini-course. I had a great experience. Before I knew it I was cutting college classes to attend Relief Society. I enjoy and appreciate Relief Society because through the vehicle of this auxiliary I can learn, stretch my spirit, reach my potentials, share my talents and growth. I love Relief Society. I wouldn't miss it! Through it I have a happy heart, a happy family, a happy home. What more could a woman ask for? I am liberated to the very soul."

As is true in many Relief Societies, I've been taught by excellent teachers who can walk with the very best in the Church. A typical Relief Society lesson is thoroughly prepared and beautifully presented. Through them I have laughed and cried, repented and rededicated myself. I have been excited and inspired, and returned home filled.

Though I could stay home and read a good book and certainly increase my knowledge, the thoughts which come to me in that solitary setting rarely compare to the ideas and feelings I get in a Relief Society group. The stimulation gained there is invaluable.

The entire world is our text through the cultural refinement lessons. Through these lessons women of the Church become conversant in the history, traditions, music, art, and literature in many lands and the progress of the Church there. Through knowledge comes understanding, and we have learned much about understanding our neighbors across the world.

Through the cultural refinement aspect of Relief Society, women of the Church are exposed to the contributions of great artists, composers, and writers. Appropriate visual materials and recordings bring the masters' works right to us and into our lives.

Cultural refinement lessons have distinctly practical applications. A sister from Provo, Utah, says that she was once asked to sing a lullaby to her children as part of one of these lessons and then to teach it to them. The song has become a permanent part of comforting babies at their home.

Once a month there is a short meeting for visiting teachers wherein they are instructed and inspired in their callings. The timely message given there is to be shared with the sisters of the ward as they make their monthly visits. In some instances, this is the only spiritual message these women hear during the month. And as accounts in a later chapter point out, this is often the beginning of full Church activity for these sisters and their families.

The importance of both the visiting teaching messages and the regular lessons can't be emphasized enough, for there are powerful forces at work in the world today attempting to destroy the God-given role of women. From Relief Society lessons I gain fortification against these treacherous means. The principles taught there give me a basis on which to judge social issues by learning to weigh and measure philosophies of the world against eternal truths. The social relations lessons, particularly, provide this for me. Through them we are reminded of what is most precious and important, what really matters most. They help us keep our perspective in a world of conflict and confusion. Furthermore, the social skills we learn there help us to relate in a more positive way to the people around us. By learning to be at our best, we are able to bring out the best in others.

I overheard a group of middle-aged women reassuring each other that during their child-rearing years they had never neglected their children. That's good, I thought, but I wondered how many of them went a few steps further and enriched the lives of their children. That's where great motherhood enters in. And through mother education lessons in Relief Society, we learn a great deal about bringing that dimension into our family living. In these lessons I am instructed, reminded, and motivated to use the best techniques known for child guidance. The Lord always makes available to us what we need; and in this complicated age, in which temptations and pitfalls surround children, mothers need the inspired lesson course of mother education.

One mother expresses thankfulness for these lessons in Relief Society by saying that she was reared in a home where children were rarely seen and never heard; but, because of the mother education classes, she has learned to play with her children, enjoy them, love them, and provide the proper environment to help them reach their full potential as people.

A Relief Society member in Arizona feels that the mother education lessons do more to help her remember and apply what she already knows than to teach her anything new. "For instance," she says, "I need all the refresher courses I can get on being a good listener to my children. Every time this topic comes up in a class, I return home to do a better job for a few more days."

The crowning point of the Relief Society agenda is the spiritual living lesson. As our purpose and destiny are discussed, the teachings of all the other lessons come into focus through this one. Here we are taught how to build a relationship with Jesus Christ which will sustain us regardless of what life brings. We learn that everything we know is incidental to knowing Jesus Christ and becoming like him.

This lesson is climaxed by a testimony-bearing period during which time sisters have the opportunity to express their gratitude for blessings and their thankfulness for the gospel. Women who might be too frightened to express thoughts in a larger setting find comfort and courage through their Relief Society sisters to rise to their feet and tell how they feel. This is a precious, sacred time.

Due to the rapid growth of the Church, spiritual living lessons are fulfilling a greater purpose than ever before. A sister from Montana put it this way: "I am a convert to the Church, and, even though I had a basic knowledge of the gospel through the missionary program, Relief Society has taught me the whole gospel plan. Little by little, through many years of attendance, I have gained these precepts."

As I visit various wards and stakes throughout the Church, I'm excited to see how much effective missionary work is being done through Relief Society. Countless LDS women are taking their nonmember friends and neighbors to socials and programs and are acquainting them with what we have to offer through homemaking day activities. This often provides a way into the Church for these women and their families. Through "common denominators" in women's lives, such as music, literature, handiwork, home decorating, child guidance, and time management, the door to doctrinal discussions can be opened. For instance, this incident took place in an Oregon community:

"It all started with a recipe. We had just moved to a new home and were welcomed to the neighborhood by the woman next door who had brought us a tasty Mexican dish. We all really enjoyed the food, so in thanking our neighbor for it I mentioned that I'd like a copy of the recipe. 'Oh,' she responded, 'that's one I picked up last week at Relief Society.' 'Where?' I asked. My curiosity about the strange-sounding term led me on to more and more questions and finally to regular attendance at Relief Society.

"What followed could take pages to tell, but what really matters is that my husband, our three children, and I are now grateful, active members of the Church. A simple inquiry about a recipe for a casserole has brought us the recipe for eternal life."

This is certainly not an isolated example of the far-reaching influence of the Relief Society, which nurtures charitable, giving actions within its membership and which teaches helpful and valuable skills, ideas, and concepts through its classes.

Even greater to me, however, than the value of the lessons in my life is the association with lovely, capable, righteous women. This is a "bonus" that cannot be printed in the lesson manual, but is Relief Society's greatest gift to me. I learn more from the lives of my sister Saints than I do from their lessons. It's the sisterhood at Relief Society which I love most.

I find that each session of Relief Society has its own special flavor. There is the near-perfection of the first session, the casualness of the second one, and the freshness of the Young Adults in their session. Each one has its strengths and contributions.

Organizing a Young Adult session of Relief Society was certainly an idea whose time had come. Young women of the Church are ready and eager for the program. I think it's exciting to see them get the Relief Society habit so early in their lives. I know of the special dividends which are in store for them as a result. No other group affiliation can mean as much, because no other group has the priorities, power, and potential that this priesthood-directed one has.

I'm extremely impressed with the Young Adults' abilities to lead and teach. They are way ahead of themselves. Their creativity and capabilities are exciting. They are knowledgeable and informed. They search the scriptures and are spiritual, humble, and prayerful. Certainly a great, prepared generation is growing up. They need very little help from the more mature Relief Society leaders, though the leaders are there in case they are needed. Perhaps their example and association are their contribution. Just the contact with a fine woman one day a week can make the difference in a young girl's choices the other six days.

Occasionally there is a Relief Society group, still in its infancy as an organization, in which the leadership and teaching are not outstanding — or, to put it bluntly, the calibre of the lessons and programs is mediocre. Such a group, of course, needs a great deal of help and support to make it grow. And the growth potential which is ours as individuals or groups is one of the most impressive facets of the gospel. As leaders and teachers humbly and prayerfully seek the guidance of the Lord and then allow his Spirit to work with them, they will come to see their weaknesses and be directed in overcoming them and becoming strong and effective. Then their lessons and programs will meet the usual high standard and quality of Relief Society activities.

It's been said that the members of the Church are the same everywhere, that it's the leadership which makes the difference. Instead of standing back and criticizing and complaining, a truly noble woman will give of herself to supporting and leading and building her Relief Society group. We will get out of Relief Society just what we put into it because it is **Our Own Society.**

Serving in Relief Society teaches us to work well with all types of people. A leadership position there offers a priceless course in human relations. The better we know others, the less inclined we are to criticize or gossip about them. Relief Society provides the blessed experience of mutually understanding each other and finding true joy in sisterhood.

Relief Society is not just an organization. It is **our** organization. It is you and me. This is well said by a Hawaiian sister who stated: "My appreciation for Relief Society is twofold: what I am able to gain and what I am able to give. It's when I am able to contribute something — anywhere from an item on the luncheon menu to a thought during a lesson — that I love it the most."

It's been accurately said that the teacher, not the student, learns the most. Over the years, I have been privileged to teach in almost every department of Relief Society. I will be eternally grateful for the knowledge and growth this has brought me. I love to teach. In fact, I would rather teach than eat or sleep.

While preparing the manuscript for this book I was serving as education counselor in our ward presidency, and just as the manuscript went to the publisher I was called as ward Relief Society president. Through such callings I have discovered that there is something even greater than teaching, and that is serving. Each day brings at least one heartwarming or joyous experience. Never before have I been so in love with a Church calling as I am this one. Working with and serving the sisters of our ward as a group or on a one-to-one basis has become one of the delights of my life. The assignment is a big one, but the work is easy because I believe in it, and the load is light because it's my sister I'm serving.

Yes, little children enjoy it long before they can say it. And their mothers, aunts, sisters, and grandmothers rejoice in the great program it offers. Relief Society is a gift from the Lord. It is a wise woman who accepts this gift with appreciation.

Angels in Aprons

During the winter of 1976-77, weather conditions throughout much of the world were extreme. Many areas were threatened by droughts and floods; severe storms and extremely low temperatures plagued other sections. Thousands of people were snowed in, and other thousands were cut off from electrical power and fuel. There was a great deal of suffering and concern, and because of this the First Presidency called for a Church-wide fast, that the Saints might implore the Lord to temper the elements. And he did.

As directives such as this fast are announced, word comes out from our prophet to Regional Representatives, to stake and district presidents, and then to bishops and branch presidents and Relief Society presidents who, in turn, direct home teachers and visiting teachers to the homes of every member of the Church everywhere. And within twenty-four hours, a special message can reach every member of the Church.

This understanding gives me an awesome feeling. I humbly realize that I, as a visiting teacher, am part of this marvelous organization. It is through people like me that the word of the Lord can be made known to his people, anywhere, at any time.

Each month as we visit the sisters of our districts, we can picture this great system within the Church and rejoice in the fact that **we** are the components. It's a very humbling, stimulating position to be in. Whether the word comes from the prophet or our bishop, it reflects the will of the Lord. It is our responsibility and blessing to help make it known. It's sobering to consider who we are representing and the significance of our task.

A visiting teacher is much, much more, however, than a bearer of information and messages, as important as that is. She is an angel of mercy. Whether she lives in parts of the world where her service involves dressing the dead and helping deliver babies, or in places where she runs around in tennis shoes, driving a station wagon, bearing delicious dishes, she is ministering to the needs of her sisters and their families. **She has been entrusted to watch over the homes assigned to her.** Sister Barbara Smith summed up the visiting teacher stewardship when she said, "Visiting teaching is not an assignment but a relationship."

m, which has been a favorite of
ur mission:

If Loaf, This

he words you said,
af of bread,
savory;
gesture meant to me,
er, lonely, too,
And gladdened by the sight of you.
I would repay you if I could.
Oh, yes, the bread was extra good.
(I'd like the recipe some day.)

But let me ask you, if I may,
How you acquired the finer art
Of nourishing the hungry heart?
I never had the knack somehow.
(I'd like that recipe right now.)

— Virginia Newman

Both of these recipes are available through Relief
Society. Rendering compassionate service is the primary
purpose and function of Relief Society. Our motto is
Charity Never Fails, and this is the greatest work on
earth. King Benjamin explained this by stating, "that ye
may learn that when ye are in the service of your fellow
beings ye are only in the service of your God." (Mosiah
2:17.)

Stories often come my way which tell of the great
work of love and service carried on by Relief Society sisters, particularly through the visiting teaching program.
There are endless reports of sisters taking food into homes

where there is illness or new babies. Countless hours are spent caring for other mothers' children or homes in times of emergency. Transportation is provided to and from doctors' offices and hospitals. New neighbors or ward members are welcomed with kind words and plates of cookies or freshly baked bread. Concern is shown to the bereaved, and thoughtful acts are extended to the lonely. People living away from their families often find that the visiting teachers become their family.

Their service is not always dramatic; usually it is just steady and sure. Visiting teachers bring with them a sweet spirit and a feeling of warmth. Perhaps a listening ear, a sympathetic heart, a word of understanding and encouragement are their contributions. To the lonely widow, their visit might be her only one for the month. A distraught mother of several small children may find this adult conversation the means of regaining her composure and perspective that day. To someone who has strayed from the Church, this might be her only contact with members. And sometimes, as in the following situation, this relationship opens the way for the person's return to activity.

"I am a visiting teacher, and I know I am blessed by this calling as much as or more than those I visit. I can think of so many wonderful women I wouldn't know if I didn't have this opportunity. Let me tell about the sharp, talented friend who became one of the best Relief Society counselors ever.

"I was a visiting teacher with a new unfamiliar name

on my list. I was told that this new family had moved into the ward and weren't active in the Church. So my partner and I knocked on the door of the luxury apartment with some apprehension that first day. She opened the door, a slim, well-dressed and very attractive woman with a warm smile. We found out as time passed that that same warm smile welcomed every one she met as a friend.

"Yes, they had just moved here from Salt Lake City. Yes, they had always been members of the Church, but, well, they were so busy with professional and social commitments that they hadn't really been to church very much and didn't really need it right now. She was witty and fun and friendly, and in the months that followed we enjoyed our visits with her. We found she had many talents and abilities. Little by little, she agreed to come to Relief Society — she missed the social life she had in Salt Lake and needed new friends. Her children started to go to Primary. Only the father seemed too busy to pay attention to the Church.

"Later, I was called to be Relief Society President. I just couldn't get her name out of my mind as I searched for counselors. The family's degree of commitment to the Church was still new and faltering, so I hesitated. After much consideration and prayer I knew she could be a good counselor.

"She was. She grew — her family grew — and I grew from sharing her basic goodness and watching her increasing awareness of what the gospel of Jesus Christ was all about.

"The family moved away a year or so later. The last time I heard from her, her husband was elders quorum president. Great happiness radiated through the written words of her letter.

"I was a visiting teacher who hesitated at the door of an inactive, unknown name and almost missed making a delightful friendship. I'm so glad that we chose to say that day, 'Hello, I'm your visiting teacher!' "

In this, as in many other cases, visiting teachers have provided the perfect cure for inactivity. A faithful sister in Missouri says: "When I was first married, I was completely inactive in the Church and painfully shy. One of the reasons I couldn't make myself go to church was that everyone was so friendly. My visiting teachers kept coming and inviting me to Relief Society. I would find one reason after another why I couldn't go. Then one day one of them called and said she would be by in twenty minutes to pick me up. And she hung up without giving me a chance to reply. I knew she was extremely busy, and I hated to have her come all that way for nothing, and yet I was too shy to call her back and tell her I couldn't go. I really agonized over the matter for a few minutes, but I made my choice and got ready so she wouldn't have to wait.

"That was the turning point in my life. I started going to Sunday School and sacrament meeting the next week. I have never missed any of them since, including Relief Society, unless I or my children are ill, which is seldom. A few years later my husband joined the Church, and needless to say the Church is now virtually our whole life. And it's all because a visiting teacher wouldn't give up and wouldn't take no for an answer."

From Minnesota comes this story: "The compassionate service which has truly meant the most to me has been the listening ear, the soft shoulder, the nonjudgmental bearing of my burdens that one or two special woman have cared enough to give me at times of real turmoil and grief. I have one son who has had two years of agony with chemical dependency. I have been so very grateful to those few sisters who have not become 'afraid' they would 'catch' our family illness and who have not made me feel that they thought I was a complete failure and a sinner. These special gospel friends have made me feel through their loving arms that the loving arms of my Savior and my Father were also about me. More than **any** amount of physical help, this emotional support which has been given in great compassion has blessed my whole family as well as myself."

Another sister shares this incident: "My baby had been hospitalized with croup and I spent the evening there with him, alone, as my husband was out of town. When I returned home I had to hear about quarreling and bickering among my five other children, and I was saddened because they hadn't pulled together in an emergency. The next day when they returned from school, they found a lovely, heart-shaped cake on the kitchen table with the message:

Love at home —
It's a special talent.

"They could hardly believe I had not left it there myself, but I had spent the day at the hospital and had not even been home. We were all touched by someone's thoughtfulness and by the appropriateness of the message. It turned out to be my visiting teachers who had called on me during their regular rounds, and finding me not home had left the cake anyway. They had no idea how timely, appreciated, and appropriate their gift was."

One woman tells how her dependable visiting teachers literally "came to her rescue" one day, and at the same time taught her (by example) the blessings to be found in Relief Society:

"I am a visiting teacher, but I haven't always been so enthusiastic about visiting teaching or, for that matter, about Relief Society. One fateful day changed my mind completely, however, and made me cherish my visiting teachers forever.

"I used to work, so I didn't go to Relief Society and didn't see my visiting teachers often. But good, patient, faithful souls that they were, they stopped at my house each month, even though they knew I probably wouldn't be home. They knew a lot about me although I hadn't bothered to get to know them very well. I certainly did nothing to encourage their visits or their friendship. In spite of all this, they took time to leave cheerful, friendly notes at my door when I wasn't home. They never missed a month.

"Since I was a working mother, mornings at my house were hectic. My youngest child went to a baby-sitter each day. I usually took her, but if she slept later I had my teenage son drop her off at the baby-sitter's on his way to school at a later hour. I gathered all her things for the day and put them by the front door so my son had only to wait for her to wake up and then bundle her off to the sitter's home nearby.

"On this terrible morning, however, my son and I didn't communicate very well. I left for work thinking he knew she was still in bed and he left later for school thinking I had taken her with me.

"My good, dear visiting teachers made their rounds that day. Once again they chose to come by my door and knock in the hope that I might be home that day. When they arrived, my baby was toddling around in the front yard, completely alone, dressed only in her pajamas.

"My visiting teachers knew something was wrong. Because they'd made the effort to find out about me, they knew where I worked. They scooped up my abandoned baby and called me at work. I arrived home shaken, horrified, and forever thankful for my visiting teachers who were led to my house on that particular day.

"From that day, I have been committed to visiting teaching and to the marvelous Relief Society program which encourages us to be sisters in deed as well as word. I reordered my life so that I could be a full-time mother. Now I partake fully of the Relief Society blessings."

Another timely act on the part of visiting teachers is described by this Utah sister: "I was busy stirring up a double batch of spaghetti sauce and making preparations for a meeting that evening. We were new in the ward, and I knew very few of my neighbors. Just moments after I had patted my little nine-month-old boy on the head and placed him in his walker, I heard him scream. Turning around, I found that he had pulled the cord of the electric frying pan and spilled the boiling sauce in his lap. I snatched him up and tore the hot, soaked clothing off him, only to find that his skin was coming off too. My head started to pound. How could I possibly handle this and care for my other little children too?

"Just then the doorbell rang. I had never seen the two women before, but I knew they were my visiting teachers. One was a nurse. They took one look at the situation, sent me to the drugstore for supplies and cared for my screaming baby until I returned. Removing me from the home for those few minutes helped me to relax and to be able to handle the care of my little boy so much more calmly. No one can ever convince me that the Lord did not send those angels to me that afternoon."

One time I had a terribly painful bursitis attack in my shoulder and upper arm which really limited my activities. Early one morning the Relief Society presidency stopped by. After sizing up the situation they didn't say, "Is there anything we can do?" I would have quickly said, "No, thank you" to that. (Such an offer is perhaps well intended but quite useless. It's hard to ask for help.) Instead, one of them asked what I planned to do next. I mentioned I was going to put my hair in rollers, as best I could. She immediately sat me down and did that for me. It was a simple thing, but I'll never forget it.

A sister from the Midwest shares this incident: "I spent five months in the hospital last year, and I can't begin to list all of the help my family received from our visiting teachers. In fact, the sisters in the ward were sensational in their assistance during this time. Knowing that my family was well cared for, I was able to concentrate my energy and thoughts on recovering."

A central Utah Relief Society member relates the following: "My husband was in Thailand. I had five children seven years of age and under. Following my homecoming after emergency surgery, my visiting teachers organized four meals for me and my little ones. They wouldn't take 'No, thank you' for an answer — the food just kept coming. Those angels in aprons! One time a thoughtful sister anonymously made a lovely maternity dress for me. What a thrill it was to look out in the congregation and know that each and every sister was capable of such compassion."

There are times when it is the intent, rather than the act, which counts, as this incident related by a young woman illustrates: "I had two delightful visiting teachers, both in their eighties. After I helped them down my front steps at the close of their visit, they wanted to know if there was anything they could do to help me!"

"In December our five-week-old son died of multiple heart deformities," tells one sister. "My dear visiting teachers were in constant contact during the hospital stay and funeral arranging. They arranged for dinners to be brought in and then went through the trouble every night for five nights to pick up each course and bring it to our home, fifteen miles away, so that this could be a private time for us. On the day of the funeral we returned home to a beautifully set dinner table and a hot meal in the oven. We'll always hold this memory as a very sacred time."

Another woman reports the gospel in action in her life:

"We were preparing for the first of our children to marry. I work part time and was not taking off work until the week before the wedding. There were many things to do that week. My time was planned to the limit with sewing, food preparation, and decorating for the event. On Monday morning, my first day off, another daughter was injured in an automobile accident and was hospitalized for three days. So I spent the first half of that week at the hospital with her.

"The Relief Society presidency called immediately and offered to help. It wasn't until Tuesday that I was even able to return the call. The president convinced me that I did need help, so I spent a few minutes considering which things I could have others do for us and then I called her back. Then I organized the sewing materials and food items so she could pick them up and distribute them to sisters who had offered help. By the end of the week when we held the reception, the Relief Society sisters had made two dresses, and prepared candied walnuts and two hundred crepes. Our family was able to accomplish the rest of the sewing and food preparations. The reception that Saturday evening was exceptionally lovely. In a way, I think we enjoyed it more and those who came enjoyed it because so many had had a hand in its success. Incidentally, my injured daughter was able to be there and even stand by her sister in the line, though her face was badly swollen and full of stitches."

To me, the point of that story is not only that the Relief Society sisters helped at a time of crisis, but that the woman in the dilemma allowed them to do so! How can others serve if we refuse to be served? Compassionate service works both ways. Not only should we give, but it is part of the gospel plan to receive when it's our turn. Just as it is wrong to be overly dependent on others, it is also an error to try to be too self-sufficient. It's good when someone feels secure enough to accept help. That is a sign of maturity and is in keeping with the true spirit of service.

This spirit of service, however, is not necessarily an inherent quality; sometimes it has to be learned or cultivated. Patricia W. Higbee supports this idea in her **Ensign** article (October 1978), "Relief Society Keeps Me Singing":

"Since Relief Society proclaims service to mankind as one of its reasons for existence, my own feelings about service have certainly improved.

"Some years ago, for instance, a brother in our ward mentioned that his wife and several of their children had the flu. I sympathized and asked routinely if I could do anything to help. He surprised me by saying, 'Yes, you could bring our dinner tomorrow night.'

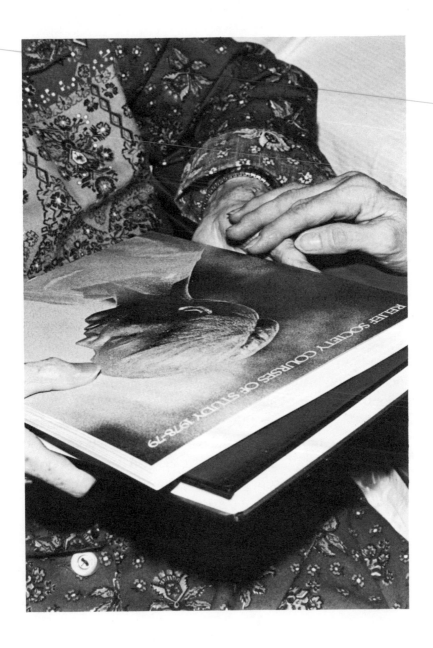

"All the next day I complained about spending my valuable time preparing a meal for his family when he was well and perfectly able to feed them himself. What a contrast that was to the happy feeling I experienced recently while preparing dinner for the family of a sister who was recuperating from surgery.

"What happened between these two experiences to change my attitude? Discussions in Relief Society about compassionate service have helped; the examples of joyful service in our ward have been even more influential. So many sisters are anxious to serve that in some instances it seems one practically has to sign a waiting list."

A friend of mine who lived across the city at one time said her ward members made absolutely no attempt at compassionate service. For some reason, no one seemed to be doing anything for anyone else. This disappointed and disturbed her, but she realized that such a pattern need not limit her activities. As a team of one she visited people who were lonely or ill and made an effort to share food or extend other thoughtful gestures wherever possible. Some months later she had to undergo surgery, and some of the people she had once called on came to see her, bearing offerings from their kitchens. She had cast her bread upon the water, so to speak, and she felt it was coming back as cake — much sweeter because she realized that through her example others were finding joy in service. Now, covered dishes are being carried from home to home throughout the neighborhood whenever there is a need, and the Relief Society sisters are leading the way in true service in the ward. This sister has since moved from that ward, but her influence will long be felt there. One person can make a difference.

There is another vital dimension of service which must not be overlooked. Sometimes it can be very discouraging and demoralizing to constantly be on the receiving end. Through a well-developed Relief Society program, opportunities for service can be extended to sisters who otherwise would have no way to give and serve. One sister, who had not been able to accept responsibility in the ward because of personal problems, was overjoyed when asked to prepare a centerpiece each week for the table in the Relief Society room. A seventy-five-year-old sister graciously agreed to make bibs for new babies born in the ward, the first Church assignment of her life! A shut-in finds some happiness through serving on several telephone-calling committees. Another sister prepares typed copies of recipes for the foods served on homemaking day, for compilation and distribution to the sisters of her ward. A life was revitalized when a sister was asked to be responsible for tape recording the lessons and then distributing the cassette tapes to shut-ins.

Relief Society sisters are angels in aprons, bearing vital messages, extending helping hands, or creating opportunities. And the Lord told us how much this matters when he stated, "Inasmuch as ye have done it unto one of the least of these my brethren, ye have done it unto me." (Matthew 25:40.)

That Relief Society Habit

When you say to the dentist's receptionist, "No, I can't go in on Wednesday morning — that's Relief Society"; or tell the repairman, "I cannot have you come Tuesday — please make it another day"; or you say, "Oh, I'm sorry, but I won't be able to go to the theatre with you Wednesday evening; I reserve that time for Relief Society" — you are converted and committed to Relief Society attendance and service. It ranks high on your list of priorities. Nothing short of an emergency or illness interferes with your attendance and participation. You have the Relief Society habit.

Habits either weaken or strengthen us, make or

break us. In fact, as insignificant as some appear in their early stages, habits can determine our destinies because the right kind of habits can exalt us. Relief Society is a good habit. It leads us in the right direction.

On the occasion of the Relief Society Centennial in 1942, President Heber J. Grant made this statement:

> Members should permit no other affiliation either to interrupt or to interfere with the work of the Relief Society. . . . We urge all sisters to take these things to heart and to cooperate in continuing the Relief Society in its position of the greatest and most efficient women's organization in the World. (A Century of Relief Society, published by the General Board of Relief Society, 1942, page 7.)

In September 1975, the First Presidency sent a circular letter to stake and mission presidents concerning the importance of attendance at Relief Society. The following excerpt from that letter sets forth the blessings that come through participation in this program:

> We note from our reports that the Relief Society meetings are not being well attended by some of our sisters. This organization, as you know, was given to the women of the Church by revelation to the Prophet Joseph Smith for the purpose of providing a unity and strength that would fortify our wives and mothers. This organization complements the priesthood training given to the brethren. May we request that you strongly endorse to the heads of families in your stake or mission that their wives regularly attend the ward or branch Relief Society meetings for the strength which this will provide to the family. We would also like to recommend that our single sisters

be encouraged to attend the Relief Society meetings which are organized for them.

President Kimball and his counselors added that in giving emphasis to the Relief Society program "our sisters will be better prepared to serve in their families, wards or branches, and communities."

Elder Boyd K. Packer, in his October 1978 conference address, said:

> Now to the sisters in the Church I say that attendance at Relief Society, in an important way, is not really optional.
>
> It is as obligatory upon a woman to draw into her life the virtues that are fostered by the Relief Society as it is an obligation for the men to build into their lives the patterns of character fostered by the priesthood.
>
> Recently I listened to several sisters discuss Relief Society. One young woman said, "We find it so difficult to interest both the older and the younger women. If we have a lesson or project the younger women are interested in, the older women do not come. It's so hard to get something to please everyone."
>
> Sisters, to me there is something pathetic about those of our sisters who sit at home waiting to be **enticed** to Relief Society. That is not right!
>
> When faithful sisters pray and work and make a worthy presentation, they deserve your support. Just to have you attend is a great help.
>
> Some sisters, it appears, seem to pore over the offering of Relief Society like a fussy diner searching a menu for something to excite the taste.
>
> Sisters, it is your duty to attend Relief Society, just

as it is the duty of the brethren to attend their priesthood meetings.

I've heard some sisters say, "I don't attend Relief Society because I just don't get anything out of it."

If you are absenting yourself from Relief Society because "you don't get anything out of it," tell me, dear sister, what is it that you are putting into it? . . .

I endorse the Relief Society without hesitation, for I know it to have been organized by inspiration from Almighty God. It has been blessed since its organization. I know that it is a rising, and not a setting, sun. I know that the light and the power that emanates from it will increase, not decrease.

(From the October 1978 General Conference address "The Relief Society," by Elder Boyd K. Packer, published in the **Ensign**. For complete talk see **Ensign**, November, 1978, pages 7-9.)

A March 11, 1978, **Church News** editorial reads in part:

The Church of Jesus Christ of Latter-day Saints has sponsored the advancement of women from its very outset. It was the Prophet Joseph Smith who set forth the ideas for womanhood. He advocated liberty for women in the purest sense of that word and he gave them liberty to fully express themselves — as mothers, as nurses for the sick, as proponents of high community ideals, and as protectors of good morals.

What more can any woman want for herself? What more could any man want for his wife? What more could any man want than to match that standard in his own conduct?

The Prophet Joseph gave us the Relief Society organization to advance these high purposes for Latter-day Saint women. That society today is a world-wide movement, holding membership in national and world organizations for the advancement of women.

It does not indulge in any of the extreme notions which some adopt. It is a wisely governed organization, presided over by the women themselves. And it is spiritual in its deepest concept.

It teaches faith in God and affirms that the glory of God is intelligence. Hence it promotes intelligence, education, high ideals of conduct and the building of strong homes and families.

Every Latter-day Saint woman should be a member of that society, should accept its program, and benefit thereby. Every man should encourage his wife and daughters to become affiliated with it. It is a mighty organization for the good of women themselves, but also for the blessing of families and whole communities.

As I've already stated, I love Relief Society with all my heart. I believe in it. Next to being at home with my husband and children, I am happier being involved in Relief Society-centered activities than in anything else. I have that Relief Society habit.

The Relief Society is the counterpart to the priesthood. Its purpose and powers will be eternal. Marvelous things, at the hands of the sisters, are in store. I want to be part of this.

Relief Society is

— a busy mother talking on the phone with a baby in her arms and her eye on dinner cooking on the stove.

— the presidency making twenty-one calls in a week to

visit the sick and the lonely.

— saying yes to the bishopric when you just know you cannot do the job and then finding out to your amazement that with the help of the Lord you did the job.

— lessons and helps with homemaking and child guidance. It's knowing that having some heaven in our homes now can mean having our homes in heaven later on.

— being ill and graciously accepting the kindnesses extended and thereby experiencing true sisterhood.

— writing original words and music for the fall social and feeding a hundred women on just thirty dollars.

— singing in public for the first time.

— learning and growing through the wisdom and experience of sisters of all ages and backgrounds.

— rushing home from a meeting so you can get to another one.

— the visiting teachers, when the wind howls or the snow is deep, bringing a word of cheer and encouragement.

— bearing testimony to the goodness of the Lord and making a declaration of faith in him and his works.

— welcoming the new neighbors with a plate of cookies.

— being reminded of what is feminine and learning how to improve our nature rather than change it.

— fifty-four children under the age of five happily learning and playing together through the nursery program.

— allowing the perspective of various teachers to expand and enlighten your own understanding.

— a daily phone call to the widow next door and being available for help at any time.

— a growing garden, fruit in a bottle, and homemade bread and jam.

— carefully sewing a nightgown for a welfare assignment.

— a tear in the eye and a tug at the heart during a beautiful lesson.

— glowing with pride as a nineteen-year-old daughter is called to serve in a Relief Society presidency.

— many sisters spending many hours serving the Lord and one another.

Yes, Relief Society is all this and much, much more. It is the gospel of Jesus Christ working in the lives of its members.

It's choosing this day to serve the Lord.

It's serving and doing, sharing and caring.

It's studying and believing, teaching and knowing.

It's truth and testimony, dedication and devotion.

It's prayer and purpose, progress and peace.

It's keeping the commandments, being committed to the Lord.

It's knowing of the Lord's love for us and rejoicing in the special program designed for his daughters.

It's working hand in hand with the priesthood for our exaltation.

It's building a home to last forever.

Most of all, Relief Society is you and me, working our way in the divine plan for our immortality and eternal life.

Book designed and composed by Bailey-Montague and Associates
in Tiffany Light with display lines in Garamond Regular Italic
Printed by Publishers Press
on 70# Bookcraft Publishers Antique
Bound by Mountain States Bindery
on Kivar 5, Royal Purple, Kidskin